HEART OF THE HOME
Postcard Collection

SUSAN BRANCH

D1403303

LITTLE, BROWN AND COMPANY

Boston · New York   *Toronto · London*

FIRST EDITION

ISBN 0-316-10661-5

♥   ♥   ♥

These postcards are reproduced from Heart of the Home,
Vineyard Seasons, Love from the Heart of the Home, &
the Heart of the Home Calendars.

10 9 8 7 6 5 4 3 2 1

Published simultaneously in Canada by Little, Brown
& Company (Canada) Limited

Printed in Singapore

Here at the frontier, there are falling leaves,

Although my neighbors are all

Barbarians,

And you, you are

a thousand miles

away . . .

There are always

two cups at my table.

Anon. T'ang Dynasty 618–906 A.D.

"Your cup! I miss you."

POSTCARD

Hi!

Just to prove the art of letter writing is not dead — a postcard for you! I've discovered that if I want to receive letters, I have to write them, & I definitely love letters! Phone calls are nice but a letter is forever. I have a basket that has a lid on it & inside I keep my favorite bits of correspondence, funny postcards, baby announcements, great letters & special valentines, & then I have a file where I keep my love letters & all other special letters in my life — all sweet memories I couldn't bear to part with.

It just takes a moment to say Hi to old friends & keep them from slipping out of your life — old friends are hard to come by! 💜 💜 💜

Well, I'm running out of space — having a WONDERFUL time! Wish you were here! With love, Susan Branch

LOVE
USA

12 APR 1994

To:
You, my sweet

Somewhere, over the rainbow

The World

2001

Now in a cottage built of lilacs and laughter
I know the meaning of the words 'ever-after'.

POLKA DOTS & MOONBEAMS

"THEREFORE ALL SEASONS SHALL BE SWEET TO THEE ..."

♥ Samuel Taylor Coleridge

"One morning we ran into a neighbor at the store and she asked brightly,

'What was it at your house?'

'Fourteen below,' we replied. Her face fell. 'We had minus twelve,' she said, and you could see that her day was ruined."

♥ Richard Ketchum

CHEESECAKE

325° Serves Eight

My dear friend Laney gave me this recipe about 15 years ago and I still haven't tried one that's better ~ It's a perfect cheesecake and requires no frills.

crust

2½ c. graham cracker crumbs
¾ c. melted butter

Combine and press into a buttered 9 in. pie plate, building up sides.

filling

1 8 oz. pkg. cream cheese, softened
½ c. sugar
1 tbsp. lemon juice
½ tsp. vanilla extract
dash salt
2 eggs

Beat softened cream cheese till fluffy. Gradually blend in sugar, lemon juice, vanilla, and salt. Add eggs, one at a time; beat after each. Pour filling into crust. Bake at 325° for 25-30 min., till set.

topping

1½ c. sour cream
3 tbsp. sugar
¾ tsp. vanilla

Combine all ingredients and spoon over top of hot cheesecake. Bake 10 min. longer. Cool ~ Chill several hours.

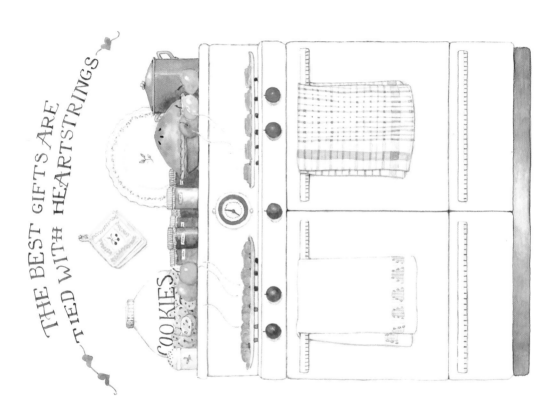

THE BEST GIFTS ARE TIED WITH HEARTSTRINGS

POPOVERS

400° Makes 12

These will pop up and over the top of the muffin pan ~ Serve them with marmalade and jam.

3 eggs
1½ c. milk
1 Tbsp. melted butter
1 tsp. salt
1½ c. unbleached flour

Butter 12 cups in muffin pans. Beat all ingredients together until smooth. Fill muffin pans 2/3 full. Bake at 400° for 45 minutes. Take them out and slit the tops ~ return to the oven for 5-10 minutes. Serve them in a large basket wrapped in a pretty cloth.

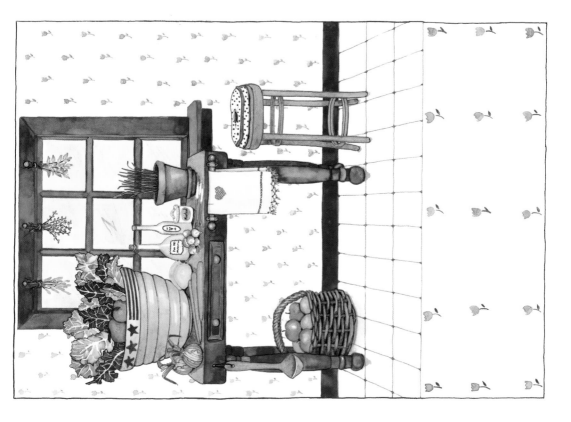

SUMMER TOMATOES

Serves Four

My grandma used to make this for us with the wonderful fresh tomatoes from her garden. Don't bother with it unless you have the firm, vine-ripened tomatoes of summer. ♥

3 tbsp. butter
1 med. onion, minced
4 good tomatoes, halved

2 tbsp. basil, minced
2/3 c. heavy cream
fresh pepper

Sauté the onions slowly in the butter till soft & golden. Put the tomatoes in the pan, cut side down, & sauté 5–7 min. Pierce skin with fork, turn them, sprinkle with basil. Cook 5 more min. Pour cream around tomatoes & boil. Add pepper to taste. Spoon sauce onto plates, set tomato in center & serve. ♥

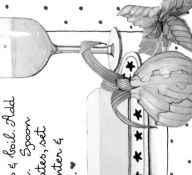

"NO HUMAN la la la WOULD ENJOY MY SINGING

ONLY MAYBE AN OLD HOUSE

THAT CAN'T BE CHOOSY."

Jessamyn West

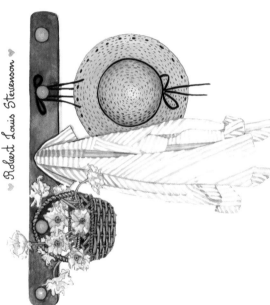

"Go, little book, and wish to all
Flowers in the garden, meat in the hall,
A bin of wine, a spice of wit,
A house with lawns enclosing it,
A living river by the door,
A nightingale in the sycamore!"

❦ Robert Louis Stevenson ❦

THEREFORE ALL SEASONS SHALL BE SWEET TO THEE…"

♥ Samuel Taylor Coleridge

"One morning we ran into a neighbor at the store and she asked brightly,

"What was it at your house?"

"Fourteen below," we replied. Her face fell. "We had minus twelve," she said, and you could see that her day was ruined."

♥ Richard Ketchum

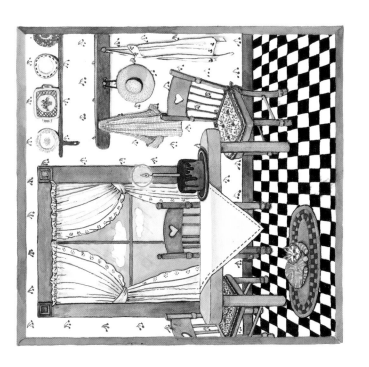

"If you cannot imagine a woman with love of you, fill her above the brim with love of herself—all that runs over will be yours."

♥ Charles Caleb Colton

CHEESE CAKE

350° Serves Eight

My dear friend Laney gave me this recipe about 15 years ago and I still haven't tried one that's better ~ It's a perfect cheesecake and requires no frills.

crust

2½ c. graham cracker crumbs
¾ c. melted butter

Combine and press into a buttered 9 in. pie plate, building up sides.

filling

1 8 oz. pkg cream cheese, softened
½ c. sugar
1 tbsp. lemon juice
½ tsp. vanilla extract
dash salt
2 eggs

Beat softened cream cheese till fluffy. Gradually blend in sugar, lemon juice, vanilla, and salt. Add eggs, one at a time, beat after each. Pour filling into crust. Bake at 325° for 25-30 min., till set.

topping

1½ c. sour cream
3 tbsp. sugar
¾ tsp. vanilla

Combine all ingredients and spoon over top of hot cheese-cake. Bake 10 min. longer. Cool ~ Chill several hours.

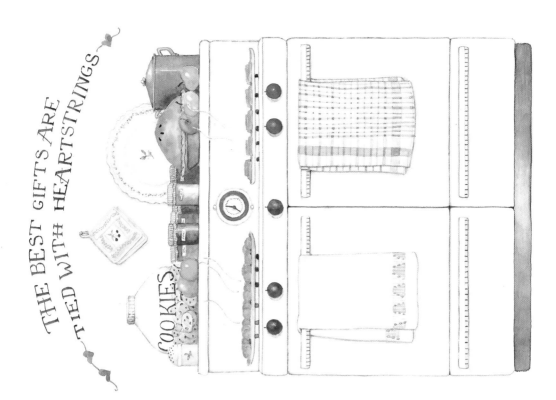

THE BEST GIFTS ARE TIED WITH HEARTSTRINGS

POPOVERS

400° Makes 12

These will pop up and over the top of the muffin pan ~ Serve them with marmalade and jam.

3 eggs
1½ c. milk
1 Tbsp. melted butter
1 tsp. salt
1½ c. unbleached flour

Butter 12 cups in muffin pans. Beat all ingredients together until smooth. Fill muffin pans ⅔ full. Bake at 400° for 45 minutes. Take them out and slit the tops ~ return to the oven for 5-10 minutes. Serve them in a large basket wrapped in a pretty cloth.

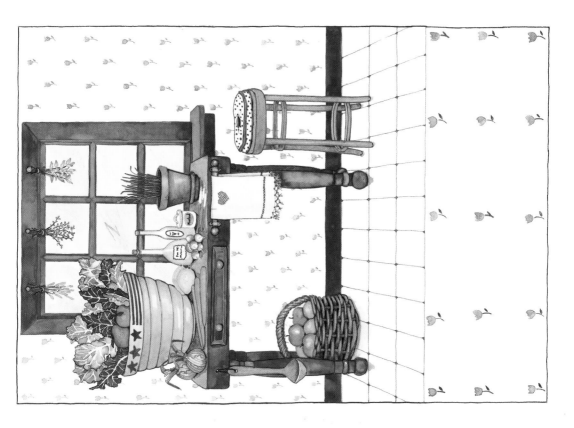

SUMMER TOMATOES

Serves Four

My grandma used to make this for us with the wonderful fresh tomatoes from her garden. Don't bother with it unless you have the firm, vine-ripened tomatoes of summer. ♥

3 tbsp. butter
1 med. onion, minced
4 good tomatoes, halved

2 tbsp. basil, minced
⅔ c. heavy cream
fresh pepper

Saute the onions slowly in the butter till soft & golden. Put the tomatoes in the pan, cut side down, & saute 5~7 min. Pierce skin with fork, turn them, sprinkle with basil. Cook 5 more min. Pour cream around tomatoes & boil. Add pepper to taste. Spoon sauce onto plates, set tomato in center & serve. ♥

"SUMMER AFTERNOON—

'SUMMER AFTERNOON:'

to me those have always been the
two most beautiful words in
the English language."

♡ Henry James

"NO HUMAN WOULD ENJOY MY SINGING ONLY MAYBE AN OLD HOUSE THAT CAN'T BE CHOOSY."

♥ Jessamyn West

la la la la la

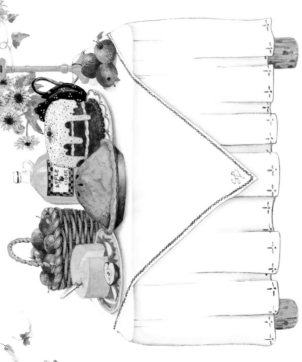

A LITTLE SEASON
OF LOVE & LAUGHTER

Listen! The wind is rising, and the air is wild with leaves,
We have had our summer evenings, now for October eves!

— Humbert Wolfe

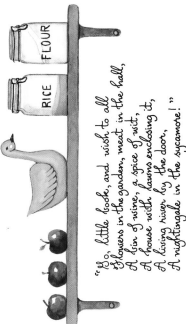

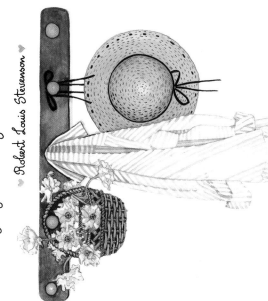

"Go, little book, and wish to all
Flowers in the garden, meat in the hall,
A bin of wine, a spice of wit,
A house with lawns enclosing it,
A living river by the door,
A nightingale in the sycamore!"

♥ Robert Louis Stevenson ♥